MAD LIBS®

WINTER GAMES
MAD LIBS

by Roger Price & Leonard Stern
with Brian Clark

MAD LIBS
An imprint of Penguin Random House LLC, New York

First published in the United States of America by Mad Libs, an imprint of
Penguin Random House LLC, New York, 2005

This edition published by Mad Libs, an imprint of Penguin Random House LLC, New York, 2021

Mad Libs format and text copyright © 2005, 2021 by Penguin Random House LLC

Concept created by Roger Price & Leonard Stern

Cover illustration by Scott Brooks

Visit us online at penguinrandomhouse.com.

Printed in the United States of America

ISBN 9780843116519
1 3 5 7 9 10 8 6 4 2
COMR

MAD LIBS®
INSTRUCTIONS

MAD LIBS® is a game for people who don't like games! It can be played by one, two, three, four, or forty.

• RIDICULOUSLY SIMPLE DIRECTIONS

In this tablet you will find stories containing blank spaces where words are left out. One player, the READER, selects one of these stories. The READER does not tell anyone what the story is about. Instead, he/she asks the other players, the WRITERS, to give him/her words. These words are used to fill in the blank spaces in the story.

• TO PLAY

The READER asks each WRITER in turn to call out a word—an adjective or a noun or whatever the space calls for—and uses them to fill in the blank spaces in the story. The result is a MAD LIBS® game.

When the READER then reads the completed MAD LIBS® game to the other players, they will discover that they have written a story that is fantastic, screamingly funny, shocking, silly, crazy, or just plain dumb—depending upon which words each WRITER called out.

• EXAMPLE (*Before* and *After*)

"_____!" he said _____
      EXCLAMATION   ADVERB

as he jumped into his convertible _____ and
                                            NOUN

drove off with his _____ wife.
                      ADJECTIVE

"_____**OUCH**_____!" he said _____**HAPPILY**_____
      EXCLAMATION   ADVERB

as he jumped into his convertible _____**CAT**_____ and
                                            NOUN

drove off with his _____**BRAVE**_____ wife.
                      ADJECTIVE

In case you have forgotten what adjectives, adverbs, nouns, and verbs are, here is a quick review:

An ADJECTIVE describes something or somebody. *Lumpy, soft, ugly, messy,* and *short* are adjectives.

An ADVERB tells how something is done. It modifies a verb and usually ends in "ly." *Modestly, stupidly, greedily,* and *carefully* are adverbs.

A NOUN is the name of a person, place, or thing. *Sidewalk, umbrella, bridle, bathtub,* and *nose* are nouns.

A VERB is an action word. *Run, pitch, jump,* and *swim* are verbs. Put the verbs in past tense if the directions say PAST TENSE. *Ran, pitched, jumped,* and *swam* are verbs in the past tense.

When we ask for A PLACE, we mean any sort of place: a country or city (*Spain, Cleveland*) or a room (*bathroom, kitchen*).

An EXCLAMATION or SILLY WORD is any sort of funny sound, gasp, grunt, or outcry, like *Wow!, Ouch!, Whomp!, Ick!,* and *Gadzooks!*

When we ask for specific words, like a NUMBER, a COLOR, an ANIMAL, or a PART OF THE BODY, we mean a word that is one of those things, like *seven, blue, horse,* or *head.*

When we ask for a PLURAL, it means more than one. For example, *cat* pluralized is *cats.*

MAD LIBS® is fun to play with friends, but you can also play it by yourself! To begin with, DO NOT look at the story on the page below. Fill in the blanks on this page with the words called for. Then, using the words you have selected, fill in the blank spaces in the story.

Now you've created your own hilarious MAD LIBS® game!

FREESTYLE SKIING

OCCUPATION (PLURAL) _____

VERB ENDING IN "ING" _____

VERB _____

PART OF THE BODY _____

ADVERB _____

VERB ENDING IN "ING" _____

PLURAL NOUN _____

PLURAL NOUN _____

NUMBER _____

ADJECTIVE _____

NOUN _____

VERB _____

NOUN _____

VERB _____

ADJECTIVE _____

VERB _____

ADJECTIVE _____

SOMETHING ALIVE _____

MAD LIBS®

FREESTYLE SKIING

From the moment the downhill _____ leave the
<u>OCCUPATION (PLURAL)</u>

_____ gates until the second they _____
<u>VERB ENDING IN "ING"</u>   <u>VERB</u>

across the finish line, this Olympic event is a/an

_____-pounding experience! The skiers must
<u>PART OF THE BODY</u>

navigate a/an _____ demanding course that can include
<u>ADVERB</u>

_____ over bumpy _____ made of snow
<u>VERB ENDING IN "ING"</u>   <u>PLURAL NOUN</u>

(known as "moguls"), maneuvering around plastic _____
<u>PLURAL NOUN</u>

planted in the snow, and jumping over _____ feet in the air. If
<u>NUMBER</u>

that isn't _____ enough, while in mid-_____, the
<u>ADJECTIVE</u>   <u>NOUN</u>

skiers flip, twist, and _____! Similar acrobatics can be seen
<u>VERB</u>

during the slopestyle, half-_____, and _____ cross
<u>NOUN</u>   <u>VERB</u>

competitions, where athletes try to catch some _____
<u>ADJECTIVE</u>

air before making a clean landing. These athletes can do so many

maneuvers, watching them can make your head _____ .
<u>VERB</u>

But one thing is certain. No matter what event you watch, these

skiers are a/an _____ sight to see and are huge
<u>ADJECTIVE</u>

_____ pleasers!
<u>SOMETHING ALIVE</u>

From WINTER GAMES MAD LIBS® • Copyright © 2005, 2021 by Penguin Random House LLC

MAD LIBS® is fun to play with friends, but you can also play it by yourself! To begin with, DO NOT look at the story on the page below. Fill in the blanks on this page with the words called for. Then, using the words you have selected, fill in the blank spaces in the story.

Now you've created your own hilarious MAD LIBS® game!

ATHLETE STATS

ADJECTIVE _____

ADJECTIVE _____

NUMBER _____

PART OF THE BODY _____

SAME PART OF THE BODY _____

PLURAL NOUN _____

VERB _____

PLURAL NOUN _____

TYPE OF FOOD (PLURAL) _____

SOMETHING ALIVE (PLURAL) _____

OCCUPATION (PLURAL) _____

PLURAL NOUN _____

NOUN _____

ADJECTIVE _____

ADJECTIVE _____

PART OF THE BODY _____

TYPE OF LIQUID _____

PLURAL NOUN _____

MAD LIBS®

ATHLETE STATS

A/An _____ survey of Winter Games athletes reveals some
    ADJECTIVE

very _____ statistics:
   ADJECTIVE

1. _____ percent are ambidextrous. The right _____
   NUMBER   PART OF THE BODY

   always knows what the left _____ is doing.
                                 SAME PART OF THE BODY

2. 93 percent set impossible _____ for themselves and
                               PLURAL NOUN

   then _____ these goals.
         VERB

3. 47 percent count their calories and eat well-balanced

   _____ —observing the recommended allowance
      PLURAL NOUN

   of fresh fruit and healthy _____ for adult
                             TYPE OF FOOD (PLURAL)

   _____ .
   SOMETHING ALIVE (PLURAL)

4. Over 50 percent of Olympic _____ play musical
                          OCCUPATION (PLURAL)

   _____ , the most popular being the piano, violin, and
   PLURAL NOUN

   six-string _____ .
           NOUN

5. 73 percent have a/an _____ sense of timing and
                   ADJECTIVE

   _____ _____ -eye coordination.
     ADJECTIVE   PART OF THE BODY

6. 94 percent don't drink carbonated _____ or other
                         TYPE OF LIQUID

   sugary _____ .
       PLURAL NOUN

MAD LIBS® is fun to play with friends, but you can also play it by yourself! To begin with, DO NOT look at the story on the page below. Fill in the blanks on this page with the words called for. Then, using the words you have selected, fill in the blank spaces in the story.

Now you've created your own hilarious MAD LIBS® game!

THE FIGURE SKATER

OCCUPATION (PLURAL) _____

TYPE OF BUILDING _____

NUMBER _____

NOUN _____

VERB _____

NOUN _____

VERB _____

VERB ENDING IN "ING" _____

VERB (PAST TENSE) _____

ARTICLE OF CLOTHING _____

PART OF THE BODY _____

ADVERB _____

SILLY WORD _____

NOUN _____

NUMBER _____

PART OF THE BODY (PLURAL) _____

SOMETHING ALIVE _____

COLOR _____

MAD LIBS®

THE FIGURE SKATER

As a crowd of more than nineteen thousand _____
OCCUPATION (PLURAL)

filed into the huge skating _____, our
TYPE OF BUILDING

_____-time _____-skating champion went
NUMBER   NOUN

through her _____-up routine. The twenty-
VERB

one-_____-old champion felt her heart start to
NOUN

_____. This was the moment she had been
VERB

_____ for her whole life. She _____
VERB ENDING IN "ING"   VERB (PAST TENSE)

onto the ice, took a deep breath, and smoothed the ruffles of her

_____ as she took her starting position. Then, the
ARTICLE OF CLOTHING

music started and the champion began her routine. She gained speed

and then performed a flawless _____ loop. Next, she
PART OF THE BODY

_____ executed a/an _____ jump, followed by a
ADVERB   SILLY WORD

triple _____! With the routine finished, the crowd gave her
NOUN

a/an _____-minute standing ovation. She had won the hearts
NUMBER

and _____ of every _____ in
PART OF THE BODY (PLURAL)   SOMETHING ALIVE

the auditorium—and maybe a/an _____ medal.
COLOR

MAD LIBS® is fun to play with friends, but you can also play it by yourself! To begin with, DO NOT look at the story on the page below. Fill in the blanks on this page with the words called for. Then, using the words you have selected, fill in the blank spaces in the story.

Now you've created your own hilarious MAD LIBS® game!

OPENING CEREMONY ANNOUNCEMENT

CITY _____

COUNTRY _____

PART OF THE BODY (PLURAL) _____

NUMBER _____

NOUN _____

VERB _____

VERB (PAST TENSE) _____

VERB ENDING IN "ING" _____

CELEBRITY _____

ADJECTIVE _____

NOUN _____

OCCUPATION (PLURAL) _____

TYPE OF BUILDING _____

NOUN _____

VERB _____

NOUN _____

VERB _____

ADJECTIVE _____

MAD LIBS®
OPENING CEREMONY ANNOUNCEMENT

Welcome to beautiful _____, where everyone in
CITY

_____ is eager to host this year's Winter Games. The
COUNTRY

_____ of the world are on the _____ athletes
PART OF THE BODY (PLURAL)   NUMBER

who have come from all the corners of the _____ to
NOUN

_____ for a gold medal and the chance to have their
VERB

names _____ into the history books forever. The
VERB (PAST TENSE)

_____ ceremony will feature performances by
VERB ENDING IN "ING"

_____, _____ multimedia presentations, and, of
CELEBRITY   ADJECTIVE

course, the lighting of the Olympic _____! And soon, the
NOUN

Olympic _____ will march into the _____
OCCUPATION (PLURAL)   TYPE OF BUILDING

to represent their home country! Each with _____ in their
NOUN

heart and the desire to show the world the best that humanity has to

_____. It's going to be quite a/an _____ to
VERB   NOUN

behold! So, _____ back, relax, and join us for the
VERB

_____ drama and spectacle of the Winter Games!
ADJECTIVE

MAD LIBS® is fun to play with friends, but you can also play it by yourself! To begin with, DO NOT look at the story on the page below. Fill in the blanks on this page with the words called for. Then, using the words you have selected, fill in the blank spaces in the story.

Now you've created your own hilarious MAD LIBS® game!

WORDS FROM A SNOWBOARDING CHAMPION

PART OF THE BODY (PLURAL) _____

NOUN _____

PART OF THE BODY (PLURAL) _____

SOMETHING ALIVE (PLURAL) _____

ADJECTIVE _____

NOUN _____

ADJECTIVE _____

PART OF THE BODY _____

OCCUPATION _____

PLURAL NOUN _____

VERB _____

NOUN _____

NOUN _____

VERB _____

PLURAL NOUN _____

ADJECTIVE _____

VERB ENDING IN "ING" _____

NOUN _____

MAD LIBS®
WORDS FROM A
SNOWBOARDING CHAMPION

Most of us have watched the sport of snowboarding spring up

before our very _____. In its short history,
                  PART OF THE BODY (PLURAL)

_____-boarding has cemented itself into the
        NOUN

_____ of sporting enthusiasts around the world. Its
PART OF THE BODY (PLURAL)

simplicity appeals to _____ of all ages. All you need
                      SOMETHING ALIVE (PLURAL)

to snowboard are _____ boots, a board made of _____,
                  ADJECTIVE   NOUN

a/an _____ sense of balance, and a willingness to risk falling
      ADJECTIVE

on your _____. I am a high-school _____ who
        PART OF THE BODY   OCCUPATION

won several _____ before trying out for the Olympic
            PLURAL NOUN

snowboarding events. Many of my closest friends say I eat, drink, and

_____ snowboarding. I admit to practicing morning, noon,
        VERB

and _____, but it paid off last week when I was invited to
    NOUN

qualify for the team in the freestyle _____. This is where my
                                      NOUN

snowboarding abilities truly _____. I'm the best at inverted
                            VERB

_____, which are _____ because you're
PLURAL NOUN   ADJECTIVE

upside down while _____. Wish me _____
                  VERB ENDING IN "ING"   NOUN

out on the slopes!

From WINTER GAMES MAD LIBS® • Copyright © 2005, 2021 by Penguin Random House LLC

MAD LIBS® is fun to play with friends, but you can also play it by yourself! To begin with, DO NOT look at the story on the page below. Fill in the blanks on this page with the words called for. Then, using the words you have selected, fill in the blank spaces in the story.

Now you've created your own hilarious MAD LIBS® game!

BOBSLEDDING

PART OF THE BODY _____

ADJECTIVE _____

NOUN _____

FIRST NAME _____

PLURAL NOUN _____

NOUN _____

SOMETHING ALIVE _____

OCCUPATION _____

VERB _____

NOUN _____

PART OF THE BODY (PLURAL) _____

NOUN _____

VERB ENDING IN "ING" _____

ADJECTIVE _____

VERB _____

NUMBER _____

LETTER OF THE ALPHABET _____

NOUN _____

MAD LIBS®

BOBSLEDDING

The name "bobsledding" comes from the early racers bobbing their

_____ back and forth to gain speed. Here are some
PART OF THE BODY

_____ phrases to provide a better understanding of this
ADJECTIVE

high-_____ sport.
NOUN

- _____ -sled: a large sled made up of two
  FIRST NAME

  _____ linked together. There are two sizes, a two-
  PLURAL NOUN

  person _____ and a four- _____ sled.
  NOUN   SOMETHING ALIVE

- **Brakeman:** the last _____ to _____ into the
  OCCUPATION   VERB

  sled. The brakeman pushes a/an _____ to bring the sled
  NOUN

  to a stop and must have very strong _____ .
  PART OF THE BODY (PLURAL)

- **Driver:** the front athlete in the bob- _____ is responsible
  NOUN

  for _____ . The driver's _____ goal is to
  VERB ENDING IN "ING"   ADJECTIVE

  maintain the straightest path down the track.

- **Push time:** the amount of time required to _____ the sled
  VERB

  down the first _____ meters of a run.
  NUMBER

- **W-** _____ : abbreviation for "what happened?"
  LETTER OF THE ALPHABET

  Usually said when the _____ crashes!
  NOUN

MAD LIBS® is fun to play with friends, but you can also play it by yourself! To begin with, DO NOT look at the story on the page below. Fill in the blanks on this page with the words called for. Then, using the words you have selected, fill in the blank spaces in the story.

Now you've created your own hilarious MAD LIBS® game!

AN OLYMPIC ANTHEM

PLURAL NOUN _____

VERB ENDING IN "ING" _____

ADJECTIVE _____

VERB _____

PART OF THE BODY _____

SILLY WORD _____

VERB _____

NOUN _____

OCCUPATION (PLURAL) _____

PLURAL NOUN _____

ADVERB _____

ADJECTIVE _____

ADJECTIVE _____

VERB ENDING IN "ING" _____

ADJECTIVE _____

SAME SILLY WORD _____

MAD LIBS

AN OLYMPIC ANTHEM

Here's the lyrics to the national anthem for an imaginary country:

With rivers and _____
PLURAL NOUN

_____ far and wide,
VERB ENDING IN "ING"

the sight of your _____ shores
ADJECTIVE

makes me _____ with pride!
VERB

With all my _____ and soul
PART OF THE BODY

I give West _____ my loyalty,
SILLY WORD

and promise to always _____ and protect
VERB

my home sweet _____'s sovereignty!
NOUN

May we never forget the _____
OCCUPATION (PLURAL)

who made our _____ self-evident!
PLURAL NOUN

And may we _____ defend our right to
ADVERB

a/an _____ and fair government.
ADJECTIVE

For our country is _____ and beautiful
ADJECTIVE

from sea to _____ sea!
VERB ENDING IN "ING"

And that's why through _____ and thin
ADJECTIVE

a citizen of West _____ is who I want to be!
SAME SILLY WORD

MAD LIBS® is fun to play with friends, but you can also play it by yourself! To begin with, DO NOT look at the story on the page below. Fill in the blanks on this page with the words called for. Then, using the words you have selected, fill in the blank spaces in the story.

Now you've created your own hilarious MAD LIBS® game!

HOCKEY FACE-OFF

NOUN _____

COLOR _____

PART OF THE BODY _____

NOUN _____

TYPE OF BUILDING _____

NOUN _____

OCCUPATION _____

PART OF THE BODY _____

VERB (PAST TENSE) _____

ADVERB _____

ADJECTIVE _____

SOMETHING ALIVE (PLURAL) _____

ADJECTIVE _____

ADVERB _____

EXCLAMATION _____

VERB ENDING IN "ING" _____

NOUN _____

NOUN _____

MAD LIBS®

HOCKEY FACE-OFF

If you dream of becoming an Olympic hockey player, you may want to

give it a second _____ before deciding to go for the
                        NOUN

_____ . Hockey is not a sport for the faint of _____!
   COLOR   PART OF THE BODY

You put your _____ in danger the moment you enter the
                  NOUN

_____ and skate onto the cold, hard _____ .
   TYPE OF BUILDING   NOUN

To be a/an _____ you have to keep your _____ in
                OCCUPATION   PART OF THE BODY

perfect shape and expect to get _____ by the other
                                    VERB (PAST TENSE)

players. A lot! But being a hockey player has its advantages. If you

become one of the _____ great players, a career in hockey will
                        ADVERB

reward you with _____ fans. These _____
                    ADJECTIVE   SOMETHING ALIVE (PLURAL)

are as _____ as the players themselves. With each goal, they
          ADJECTIVE

cheer _____ by screaming, " _____ " while
          ADVERB   EXCLAMATION

_____ their hands in the _____ . Given their
   VERB ENDING IN "ING"   NOUN

raw enthusiasm, you can see why some consider hockey to be the most

physically demanding _____ at the Winter Games.
                        NOUN

MAD LIBS® is fun to play with friends, but you can also play it by yourself! To begin with, DO NOT look at the story on the page below. Fill in the blanks on this page with the words called for. Then, using the words you have selected, fill in the blank spaces in the story.

Now you've created your own hilarious MAD LIBS® game!

UNLEASH YOUR OLYMPIC SPIRIT!

NUMBER _____

ANIMAL (PLURAL) _____

PART OF THE BODY _____

ANIMAL _____

ADVERB _____

NOUN _____

NOUN _____

SOMETHING ALIVE (PLURAL) _____

NUMBER _____

NUMBER _____

ADJECTIVE _____

OCCUPATION (PLURAL) _____

NOUN _____

A PLACE _____

VERB ENDING IN "ING" _____

VERB (PAST TENSE) _____

OCCUPATION (PLURAL) _____

NOUN _____

MAD LIBS®
UNLEASH YOUR
OLYMPIC SPIRIT!

Of all the demonstration sports ever presented at the Winter Games,

dogsled racing was my favorite. Watching these beautiful

_____-legged _____ courageously pulling their
　　NUMBER　　　　　ANIMAL (PLURAL)

sled across the snow really tugged at my _____-strings. The
　　　　　　　　　　　　　　　　　　PART OF THE BODY

rules for _____-sled racing are _____simple—
　　　　　ANIMAL　　　　　　　　　　ADVERB

the first team to cross the finish _____ wins the gold
　　　　　　　　　　　　　　　　NOUN

_____. A dogsled team consists of fourteen Siberian
　　NOUN

_____, each weighing approximately _____
SOMETHING ALIVE (PLURAL)　　　　　　　　　　　NUMBER

pounds and each able to pull _____ times its weight. These
　　　　　　　　　　　　　NUMBER

beautiful and _____ dogs are trained to respond to the
　　　　　ADJECTIVE

commands of their _____. The driver stands on a/an
　　　　　　　OCCUPATION (PLURAL)

_____ at the rear of the sled while guiding the dogs through
　　NOUN

(the) _____. It's amazing to see the dogs and their driver all
　　A PLACE

_____ together, like a well-_____
VERB ENDING IN "ING"　　　　　　　　　　VERB (PAST TENSE)

machine. The bond displayed between humans and these canine

_____ during these races is proof that dogs are truly man's
OCCUPATION (PLURAL)

best _____ .
　　NOUN

MAD LIBS® is fun to play with friends, but you can also play it by yourself! To begin with, DO NOT look at the story on the page below. Fill in the blanks on this page with the words called for. Then, using the words you have selected, fill in the blank spaces in the story.

Now you've created your own hilarious MAD LIBS® game!

THE OLYMPIC VILLAGE

TYPE OF BUILDING _____

NUMBER _____

ADJECTIVE _____

PART OF THE BODY _____

VERB ENDING IN "ING" _____

NOUN _____

VERB ENDING IN "ING" _____

OCCUPATION _____

ADJECTIVE _____

TYPE OF CONTAINER _____

PLURAL NOUN _____

NOUN _____

PLURAL NOUN _____

VERB ENDING IN "ING" _____

NOUN _____

ADVERB _____

NOUN _____

SILLY WORD _____

MAD☺LIBS®

THE OLYMPIC VILLAGE

Having a comfortable _____ away from home is
TYPE OF BUILDING

important for every Olympic athlete! Many competitors travel more

than _____ miles to compete in the games and need to have a/an
NUMBER

_____ place to lay down their _____ after
ADJECTIVE   PART OF THE BODY

a long day of cross-country _____,
VERB ENDING IN "ING"

_____ -boarding, and ice- _____ . The
NOUN   VERB ENDING IN "ING"

bedroom of each suite in the Olympic Village has a/an

_____ -size bed with a/an _____ mattress. The
OCCUPATION   ADJECTIVE

bathroom comes equipped with a hot- _____ , so
TYPE OF CONTAINER

athletes can relax their aching muscles. The Olympic Village also

provides entertainment like _____ shown on a big-screen
PLURAL NOUN

TV. Other amenities include a/an _____ -burning fireplace,
NOUN

a game room stocked with arcade _____ , and game
PLURAL NOUN

tables for _____ checkers, as well as a Ping-Pong
VERB ENDING IN "ING"

_____ . And, of course, since good nutrition is _____
NOUN   ADVERB

essential to our athletes, the Olympic Village has nine restaurants, each

with a five- _____ rating! _____ appétit!
NOUN   SILLY WORD

From WINTER GAMES MAD LIBS® • Copyright © 2005, 2021 by Penguin Random House LLC

MAD LIBS® is fun to play with friends, but you can also play it by yourself! To begin with, DO NOT look at the story on the page below. Fill in the blanks on this page with the words called for. Then, using the words you have selected, fill in the blank spaces in the story.

Now you've created your own hilarious MAD LIBS® game!

OLYMPIC SKI ADVICE

VERB ENDING IN "ING" _____

PERSON IN ROOM _____

VERB _____

ADJECTIVE _____

PLURAL NOUN _____

ADVERB _____

PLURAL NOUN _____

VERB (PAST TENSE) _____

PLURAL NOUN _____

NOUN _____

ADJECTIVE _____

PLURAL NOUN _____

PLURAL NOUN _____

ADJECTIVE _____

PLURAL NOUN _____

PLURAL NOUN _____

VERB ENDING IN "ING" _____

PART OF THE BODY _____

MAD LIBS®

OLYMPIC SKI ADVICE

According to the pioneer of downhill _____ ,

VERB ENDING IN "ING"

_____ , "When you first learn to _____ , the cost of

PERSON IN ROOM   VERB

your ski equipment should be the equal of your _____

ADJECTIVE

ability." Remember this sage advice for beginners when purchasing

your first pair of _____ . It is _____

PLURAL NOUN   ADVERB

important to take many _____ into consideration

PLURAL NOUN

before plunking down hard-_____ bucks for your

VERB (PAST TENSE)

new _____ . Your height, age, and _____ are all

PLURAL NOUN   NOUN

_____ factors to consider when selecting a pair of

ADJECTIVE

_____ that match your skills and _____ . Make

PLURAL NOUN   PLURAL NOUN

sure your skis are made of quality materials. _____

ADJECTIVE

skis made of _____ or _____ are usually

PLURAL NOUN   PLURAL NOUN

best. When it comes to learning to ski, it goes without

_____ : If you don't have the right skis, you're starting

VERB ENDING IN "ING"

off on the wrong _____ .

PART OF THE BODY

From WINTER GAMES MAD LIBS® • Copyright © 2005, 2021 by Penguin Random House LLC

MAD LIBS® is fun to play with friends, but you can also play it by yourself! To begin with, DO NOT look at the story on the page below. Fill in the blanks on this page with the words called for. Then, using the words you have selected, fill in the blank spaces in the story.

Now you've created your own hilarious MAD LIBS® game!

A GOLDEN CODE OF CONDUCT

OCCUPATION (PLURAL) _____

PLURAL NOUN _____

NOUN _____

VERB ENDING IN "ING" _____

TYPE OF EVENT (PLURAL) _____

ADJECTIVE _____

NOUN _____

PLURAL NOUN _____

TYPE OF LIQUID _____

VERB ENDING IN "ING" _____

ADJECTIVE _____

NOUN _____

PLURAL NOUN _____

PLURAL NOUN _____

VERB _____

VERB ENDING IN "ING" _____

SOMETHING ALIVE (PLURAL) _____

MAD☻LIBS®
A GOLDEN CODE OF CONDUCT

All Olympic _____ are expected to follow these
　　　　　　　OCCUPATION (PLURAL)

_____ of conduct:
PLURAL NOUN

1. All athletes must have respect for the Olympic _____,
　　　　　　　　　　　　　　　　　　　　　　　　　NOUN

    which requires _____ other competitors,
　　　　　　　　　VERB ENDING IN "ING"

    participating in the Opening and Closing _____,
　　　　　　　　　　　　　　　　　　　　　　　TYPE OF EVENT (PLURAL)

    and following the rules of _____ play.
　　　　　　　　　　　　　　　ADJECTIVE

2. All athletes must refrain from using _____ enhancing
　　　　　　　　　　　　　　　　　　　　　　NOUN

    chemicals and/or _____ and must be willing to
　　　　　　　　　　　PLURAL NOUN

    undergo random _____ tests. _____
　　　　　　　　　　TYPE OF LIQUID　　　　　　　　VERB ENDING IN "ING"

    is strictly forbidden and will result in _____ removal from
　　　　　　　　　　　　　　　　　　　　　　　ADJECTIVE

    the games.

3. All athletes must follow the laws of the host _____.
　　　　　　　　　　　　　　　　　　　　　　　　　NOUN

    This includes protecting all human _____ and
　　　　　　　　　　　　　　　　　　　　PLURAL NOUN

    following local _____ .
　　　　　　　　　　PLURAL NOUN

4. All athletes must _____ and protect the safety and well-
　　　　　　　　　　　　VERB

    _____ of their fellow _____ .
    VERB ENDING IN "ING"　　　　　　　　SOMETHING ALIVE (PLURAL)

MAD LIBS® is fun to play with friends, but you can also play it by yourself! To begin with, DO NOT look at the story on the page below. Fill in the blanks on this page with the words called for. Then, using the words you have selected, fill in the blank spaces in the story.

Now you've created your own hilarious MAD LIBS® game!

GETTING COZY
WITH CURLING

PLURAL NOUN _____

VERB ENDING IN "ING" _____

VERB _____

VEHICLE _____

NUMBER _____

NUMBER _____

OCCUPATION (PLURAL) _____

VERB ENDING IN "ING" _____

PLURAL NOUN _____

TYPE OF BUILDING _____

ADVERB _____

NOUN _____

VERB ENDING IN "S" _____

NOUN _____

ADJECTIVE _____

PLURAL NOUN _____

NOUN _____

NOUN _____

MAD☺LIBS®
GETTING COZY
WITH CURLING

Curling is an Olympic sport that involves sliding _____
_____ PLURAL NOUN

on a sheet of ice toward a target. It is similar to sports like ten-pin

_____ or like playing _____ -board on a
VERB ENDING IN "ING"   VERB

cruise _____ . _____ teams compete against each
        VEHICLE   NUMBER

other, with _____ _____ on each team. The teams
            NUMBER   OCCUPATION (PLURAL)

take turns _____ heavy granite _____
           VERB ENDING IN "ING"   PLURAL NOUN

(also called rocks) toward a target called a/an _____ .
                                                 TYPE OF BUILDING

Athletes can "curl" the stone by causing it to _____ turn as it
                                                ADVERB

slides down the slippery _____ . While the stone
                          NOUN

_____ down the ice, another team member can use
VERB ENDING IN "S"

a/an _____ to sweep the ice in front of the stone. This helps
      NOUN

the stone travel _____ and far and can help win
                 ADJECTIVE

_____ or knock the other player's stone out of the game.
PLURAL NOUN

This is a game of strategy, requiring lots of _____ and
                                              NOUN

concentration. That's why curling is sometimes described as playing

chess on a/an _____ made out of ice!
               NOUN

MAD LIBS® is fun to play with friends, but you can also play it by yourself! To begin with, DO NOT look at the story on the page below. Fill in the blanks on this page with the words called for. Then, using the words you have selected, fill in the blank spaces in the story.

Now you've created your own hilarious MAD LIBS® game!

SKI JUMPING

OCCUPATION _____

SOMETHING ALIVE _____

TYPE OF BUILDING _____

NOUN _____

ADJECTIVE _____

NOUN _____

COLOR _____

NOUN _____

ADVERB _____

NOUN _____

TYPE OF EVENT (PLURAL) _____

NOUN _____

VERB _____

PLURAL NOUN _____

PART OF THE BODY _____

NOUN _____

SILLY WORD _____

PART OF THE BODY (PLURAL) _____

MAD LIBS®

SKI JUMPING

Whether you're a/an _____ seated in the stands or
                          OCCUPATION

a/an _____ watching on television at your local
          SOMETHING ALIVE

_____ , ski jumping is an amazing sport that will
   TYPE OF BUILDING

take your _____ away. There's something so _____
              NOUN   ADJECTIVE

about a skier taking flight, soaring into the crystal-clear

_____ , against the _____ sky with
       NOUN   COLOR

_____ -capped mountains looming _____ in the
    NOUN   ADVERB

distance! _____ jumping is clearly one of the most dramatic
               NOUN

events of the Olympic _____ . There's drama in every
                         TYPE OF EVENT (PLURAL)

jump. You can't help but sit on the edge of your _____ and
                                                      NOUN

_____ your breath as adrenaline and other _____
   VERB   PLURAL NOUN

race through your _____ . Will the skier break the world
                     PART OF THE BODY

_____ ? Minutes later, the crowd is cheering,
    NOUN

" _____ !" at the top of their lungs and you have your
   SILLY WORD

answer. You've got a world champion on your _____ .
                                               PART OF THE BODY (PLURAL)

MAD LIBS® is fun to play with friends, but you can also play it by yourself! To begin with, DO NOT look at the story on the page below. Fill in the blanks on this page with the words called for. Then, using the words you have selected, fill in the blank spaces in the story.

Now you've created your own hilarious MAD LIBS® game!

SPEED SKATING

NOUN _____

ADVERB _____

PART OF THE BODY _____

OCCUPATION (PLURAL) _____

NOUN _____

NOUN _____

VERB ENDING IN "ING" _____

ADVERB _____

VERB _____

NOUN _____

PART OF THE BODY _____

PART OF THE BODY _____

VERB (PAST TENSE) _____

ARTICLE OF CLOTHING (PLURAL) _____

NOUN _____

NOUN _____

NOUN _____

MAD LIBS®

SPEED SKATING

An Olympic speed-skating _____ goes by so _____
NOUN   ADVERB

that if you blink a/an _____ , you might miss the
PART OF THE BODY

race. In every competition, skaters not only race against their fellow

_____ , but they also race against the ticking
OCCUPATION (PLURAL)

_____ . They know a fraction of a/an _____ can be
NOUN   NOUN

the difference between winning and _____ . These
VERB ENDING IN "ING"

skaters _____ live for speed! When racing, they
ADVERB

_____ with their bodies angled toward the _____
VERB   NOUN

and one _____ behind them, pressed firmly against their
PART OF THE BODY

_____ . This is done to eliminate being _____
PART OF THE BODY   VERB (PAST TENSE)

down by wind resistance. They even wear skintight

_____ to improve their speed. You can see
ARTICLE OF CLOTHING (PLURAL)

by the _____ in their eyes that they're only focused on one
NOUN

thing . . . the finish _____ . They know that each stride
NOUN

forward is one _____ closer to winning the gold!
NOUN

MAD LIBS® is fun to play with friends, but you can also play it by yourself! To begin with, DO NOT look at the story on the page below. Fill in the blanks on this page with the words called for. Then, using the words you have selected, fill in the blank spaces in the story.

Now you've created your own hilarious MAD LIBS® game!

DOUBLE LUGE

NOUN _____

PLURAL NOUN _____

OCCUPATION (PLURAL) _____

VERB (PAST TENSE) _____

PERSON IN ROOM _____

CELEBRITY _____

NOUN _____

NOUN _____

NUMBER _____

PLURAL NOUN _____

A PLACE _____

PART OF THE BODY (PLURAL) _____

PART OF THE BODY (PLURAL) _____

NOUN _____

VERB _____

PART OF THE BODY (PLURAL) _____

ARTICLE OF CLOTHING _____

PLURAL NOUN _____

MAD LIBS®

DOUBLE LUGE

Although the double _____ is thought to be relatively new,
             NOUN

it's actually one of the oldest of all winter _____.
                              PLURAL NOUN

It was enjoyed by kings, queens, and _____ who
                         OCCUPATION (PLURAL)

_____ the sport in the sixteenth century. King
VERB (PAST TENSE)

_____ was a huge fan, as was _____! *Luge*
PERSON IN ROOM   CELEBRITY

is the French word for _____. The luge travels at a/an
                        NOUN

_____-threatening speed, often exceeding _____ miles
NOUN   NUMBER

per hour. Luge athletes become virtual flying _____ from
                            PLURAL NOUN

the moment they step into (the) _____, lie flat on
                        A PLACE

their _____, and push off with their
      PART OF THE BODY (PLURAL)

_____ looking up to the sky. As they fly down the
PART OF THE BODY (PLURAL)

ice-covered _____, they _____ the luge left or right
           NOUN   VERB

by pressing their _____ against the front runners.
           PART OF THE BODY (PLURAL)

Protected only by a/an _____, they risk their
               ARTICLE OF CLOTHING

_____ until they speed across the finish line!
PLURAL NOUN

MAD LIBS® is fun to play with friends, but you can also play it by yourself! To begin with, DO NOT look at the story on the page below. Fill in the blanks on this page with the words called for. Then, using the words you have selected, fill in the blank spaces in the story.

Now you've created your own hilarious MAD LIBS® game!

JOB AD FOR AN OLYMPIC JUDGE

OCCUPATION _____

PART OF THE BODY _____

ADJECTIVE _____

ADJECTIVE _____

NUMBER _____

VERB ENDING IN "ING" _____

FIRST NAME _____

NOUN _____

VERB ENDING IN "ING" _____

NOUN _____

ADJECTIVE _____

PLURAL NOUN _____

NOUN _____

ADJECTIVE _____

PART OF THE BODY _____

VERB ENDING IN "ING" _____

EXCLAMATION _____

NUMBER _____

MAD LIBS®
JOB AD FOR AN
OLYMPIC JUDGE

Do you want to become an Olympic _____? If so, here's an
<u>OCCUPATION</u>

ad for your new favorite job:

WANTED:

Olympic judge with a keen _____ and a/an _____
<u>PART OF THE BODY</u>   <u>ADJECTIVE</u>

attention to detail. Must be _____ and fair and able to count
<u>ADJECTIVE</u>

from one to _____. Knowledge of snow _____,
<u>NUMBER</u>   <u>VERB ENDING IN "ING"</u>

_____-sledding, skiing, and _____-skating
<u>FIRST NAME</u>   <u>NOUN</u>

required. This job also requires _____ to other
<u>VERB ENDING IN "ING"</u>

countries, a comfort around a fiery _____, and experience
<u>NOUN</u>

in a/an _____-paced environment with lots of loud
<u>ADJECTIVE</u>

_____ that explode in the _____. The
<u>PLURAL NOUN</u>   <u>NOUN</u>

_____ candidate will need a thick _____ and
<u>ADJECTIVE</u>   <u>PART OF THE BODY</u>

be comfortable _____ in front of a large audience who
<u>VERB ENDING IN "ING"</u>

may yell, "_____" if they don't agree with the scores.
<u>EXCLAMATION</u>

Ability to speak _____ languages a plus!
<u>NUMBER</u>

From WINTER GAMES MAD LIBS® • Copyright © 2005, 2021 by Penguin Random House LLC

MAD LIBS® is fun to play with friends, but you can also play it by yourself! To begin with, DO NOT look at the story on the page below. Fill in the blanks on this page with the words called for. Then, using the words you have selected, fill in the blank spaces in the story.

Now you've created your own hilarious MAD LIBS® game!

SKIING DISCIPLINES

VERB ENDING IN "ING" _____

ADJECTIVE _____

PLURAL NOUN _____

ADJECTIVE _____

NOUN _____

NOUN _____

SOMETHING ALIVE (PLURAL) _____

ADJECTIVE _____

OCCUPATION (PLURAL) _____

OCCUPATION (PLURAL) _____

VERB ENDING IN "ING" _____

ADJECTIVE _____

ADJECTIVE _____

VERB _____

VERB _____

NOUN _____

MAD LIBS

SKIING DISCIPLINES

There are many different types of _____ events found
VERB ENDING IN "ING"

in the Winter Games. Each has its own _____ features and
ADJECTIVE

offers different kinds of _____ for _____ skiers.
PLURAL NOUN   ADJECTIVE

Here are some of the major types of skiing events:

- **Alpine Skiing:** Athletes in this event ski down the side of a/an

  _____ in down- _____ or slalom races. It is
  NOUN   NOUN

  practiced by extremely talented _____ .
  SOMETHING ALIVE (PLURAL)

- **Telemark Skiing:** This is a/an _____ style of skiing. It
  ADJECTIVE

  uses a turning technique admired by many _____and
  OCCUPATION (PLURAL)

  mastered by few _____ .
  OCCUPATION (PLURAL)

- **Freestyle _____:** This takes the sport of skiing
  VERB ENDING IN "ING"

  to _____ heights, using skis in many _____ ways
  ADJECTIVE   ADJECTIVE

  to _____ , _____ , and jump in midair.
  VERB   VERB

- **Nordic Combined:** This event combines a ski jump with

  cross- _____ skiing!
  NOUN

MAD LIBS® is fun to play with friends, but you can also play it by yourself! To begin with, DO NOT look at the story on the page below. Fill in the blanks on this page with the words called for. Then, using the words you have selected, fill in the blank spaces in the story.

Now you've created your own hilarious MAD LIBS® game!

COACH COMMENTS

NOUN _____

FIRST NAME _____

VERB (PAST TENSE) _____

NUMBER _____

ADJECTIVE _____

OCCUPATION _____

PLURAL NOUN _____

VERB _____

COUNTRY _____

NOUN _____

NOUN _____

VERB _____

TYPE OF BUILDING (PLURAL) _____

PLURAL NOUN _____

VERB ENDING IN "ING" _____

NOUN _____

MAD LIBS

COACH COMMENTS

Here's a conversation between a coach and her Olympic skater before

she heads into the _____ .

NOUN

Coach: _____ , this is your moment to shine! You've

FIRST NAME

_____ for _____ years and I'm so proud of all

VERB (PAST TENSE)   NUMBER

the _____ work you've done.

ADJECTIVE

Athlete: Thanks so much, _____ . It's because of all the great

OCCUPATION

_____ you've given me.

PLURAL NOUN

Coach: Now, _____ out there and show them what

VERB

_____ can do! You're the best _____ -skater in the

COUNTRY   NOUN

northern _____ . Show them how to _____ !

NOUN   VERB

Athlete: I will, coach! I'm dedicating this routine to everyone watching

from their _____ , who supported me with their love

TYPE OF BUILDING (PLURAL)

and their _____ .

PLURAL NOUN

Coach: Everyone is _____ for you! Let's go grab that

VERB ENDING IN "ING"

_____ !

NOUN

From WINTER GAMES MAD LIBS® • Copyright © 2005, 2021 by Penguin Random House LLC

MAD LIBS® is fun to play with friends, but you can also play it by yourself! To begin with, DO NOT look at the story on the page below. Fill in the blanks on this page with the words called for. Then, using the words you have selected, fill in the blank spaces in the story.

Now you've created your own hilarious MAD LIBS® game!

HISTORY OF THE WINTER GAMES

CITY _____

COUNTRY _____

NOUN _____

LETTER OF THE ALPHABET _____

NOUN _____

SOMETHING ALIVE (PLURAL) _____

NOUN _____

NUMBER _____

PLURAL NOUN _____

NUMBER _____

ADJECTIVE _____

PLURAL NOUN _____

PART OF THE BODY _____

EXCLAMATION _____

VEHICLE _____

PART OF THE BODY _____

PLURAL NOUN _____

NOUN _____

MAD LIBS
HISTORY OF THE
WINTER GAMES

The first Winter Games were held in _____ , _____ .
                                         CITY   COUNTRY

Governed by the International Olympic _____ (or
                                              NOUN

I- _____ -C), the modern Winter Olympics are a
   LETTER OF THE ALPHABET

chance for the entire _____ to come together as
                            NOUN

_____ from all nations compete for greatness and
SOMETHING ALIVE (PLURAL)

their _____ in history! Except for being interrupted by
          NOUN

World War _____ in 1940 and 1944, the Winter Games have
             NUMBER

been held at least every four _____ since their debut in the
                               PLURAL NOUN

year _____ . Over the years, new and _____ winter
        NUMBER   ADJECTIVE

_____ have been added to the games by the Olympic
PLURAL NOUN

Committee. One example is called "skeleton," where the athlete rides

_____ -first down a steep hill. _____ ! The
PART OF THE BODY   EXCLAMATION

sport is called skeleton because the metal frame of the _____
                                                            VEHICLE

originally used was said to resemble a human _____ . Other
                                               PART OF THE BODY

disciplines, like military patrol, have been removed from the

_____ and are no longer presented. To watch those, you'll
PLURAL NOUN

need a/an _____ machine!
             NOUN

MAD LIBS® is fun to play with friends, but you can also play it by yourself! To begin with, DO NOT look at the story on the page below. Fill in the blanks on this page with the words called for. Then, using the words you have selected, fill in the blank spaces in the story.

Now you've created your own hilarious MAD LIBS® game!

AWARD CEREMONIES

ADJECTIVE _____

NOUN _____

PLURAL NOUN _____

NOUN _____

OCCUPATION (PLURAL) _____

PART OF THE BODY _____

PART OF THE BODY _____

ADJECTIVE _____

PART OF THE BODY _____

ADJECTIVE _____

SOMETHING ALIVE (PLURAL) _____

VERB (PAST TENSE) _____

TYPE OF BUILDING _____

PERSON IN ROOM _____

ADJECTIVE _____

NOUN _____

PART OF THE BODY (PLURAL) _____

AWARD CEREMONIES

By far, the most touching and _____ moments of the games
                              ADJECTIVE

are the _____ ceremonies in which first-, second-, and third-
        NOUN

place _____ stand on the _____ and are presented
      PLURAL NOUN   NOUN

to the winning _____. There's hardly a dry
               OCCUPATION (PLURAL)

_____ in the stadium when the officials shake the athlete's
PART OF THE BODY

_____ and place the _____ medal around their
PART OF THE BODY   ADJECTIVE

_____. Perhaps the most memorable and meaningful
PART OF THE BODY

moment occurs when the _____ winner is handed a bouquet
                       ADJECTIVE

of _____ and the national anthem of their country
   SOMETHING ALIVE (PLURAL)

is _____ over the loudspeakers. Everyone in the whole
   VERB (PAST TENSE)

_____ is thrilled for the winner, especially the judges,
TYPE OF BUILDING

who are often former athletes like _____. When the song
                                    PERSON IN ROOM

ends, the athletes usually break into _____ smiles, lift their
                                       ADJECTIVE

_____ high in the air, and acknowledge the crowd by waving
NOUN

their _____.
      PART OF THE BODY (PLURAL)